Andrzej Kotański

POEMS ABOUT MY PSYCHIATRIST

POEMS ABOUT MY PSYCHIATRIST

by Andrzej Kotański

Translated from the Polish
and introduced by Charles S. Kraszewski

Proofreading by Richard Coombes

Publishers Maxim Hodak & Max Mendor

Introduction and English translation © 2022, Charles S. Kraszewski

© 2022, Andrzej Kotański

© 2022, Glagoslav Publications

Book cover and interior book design by Max Mendor

www.glagoslav.com

ISBN: 978-1-80484-008-5

Published by Glagoslav Publications in November 2022.
A catalogue record for this book is available from the British Library.

This book is in copyright. No part of this publication may be reproduced, stored in a retrieval system or transmitted in any form or by any means without the prior permission in writing of the publisher, nor be otherwise circulated in any form of binding or cover other than that in which it is published without a similar condition, including this condition, being imposed on the subsequent purchaser.

Andrzej Kotański

POEMS ABOUT MY PSYCHIATRIST

Translated from the Polish
and introduced by Charles S. Kraszewski

GLAGOSLAV PUBLICATIONS

Contents

INTRODUCTION: THE WRITING ON THE WALL
by *Charles S. Kraszewski* 8

POEMS ABOUT MY PSYCHIATRIST

    MY PSYCHIATRIST WENT SKIING 30
    MY PSYCHIATRIST HAD A CLAUSTROPHOBIC EPISODE . . . 31
    MY PSYCHIATRIST HAS EPISODES OF FURY 32
    MY PSYCHIATRIST HAS A LOT TO SAY TO ME 33
    MY PSYCHIATRIST SUMS UP BUENOS AIRES 34
    MY PSYCHIATRIST WON'T WRITE ME WORK-RELEASES . . 35
    MY PSYCHIATRIST'S MUMBLING 36
    I SAY TO MYSELF 37
    MY PSYCHIATRIST SAYS 38
    YOU'VE GOT TO FINALLY 39
    MY PSYCHIATRIST REPRISES HIS FAVOURITE THEME . . . 40
    ILLUSIONS ILLUSIONS ILLUSIONS 41
    MY PSYCHIATRIST CITES HIS PATIENT'S POEM 42
    MY PSYCHIATRIST IS PLAYING WITH A DOG 43
    RATE HIKE PAINFUL RATE HIKE 44
    MY CONDITION IS STABLE 45
    FOR THE LOVE OF GOD MAN 46
    FOR THE LOVE OF GOD MAN 2 47
    RELATIONSHIP TO DADDY 48
    MY PSYCHIATRIST DOESN'T KNOW WHAT TO DO WITH ME . 49
    MY PSYCHIATRIST PRETENDS THAT HE DOESN'T EXIST . . 50
    AN ADMISSION 51

MY GRANDEST ILLUSION. 52

RETURNING TO THE HERE AND NOW 53

RETURNING TO THE HERE AND NOW 2. 54

MY PSYCHIATRIST LISTENS TO JAZZ 55

IMPATIENCE 56

THE FIRST CONVERSATION. 57

I DON'T KNOW WHAT THEY MEAN 58

UNUSUAL NAMES 59

SYMPTOMS OF THE WANDERING REASON 60

REAL THERAPY REALLY 61

RETURNING TO THE HERE AND NOW 3. 62

DYSFUNCTIONAL EMANATIONS 63

WHY 64

NON-NEW YORK JAZZ 65

MY LUCIFERISM 66

MY PROMISCUITY. 67

MY ANIMA. 68

MY EVERYDAY DANDYISM 69

EVERYDAY DANDYISM 2 70

CORTE DEL LUGANEGHER 71

WE TALK ABOUT QUANTUM PHYSICS 72

PITY PARTY 73

MY PSYCHIATRIST GOES A-HUNTING 74

WE TALK ABOUT LIFE 75

WE TALK ABOUT DEATH 76

WE TALK ABOUT THE INTERNET 77

WE TALK ABOUT LOVE 78

MY PSYCHIATRIST CITES HIS PATIENT'S POEM 2. 79

WE TALK ABOUT MY EX-WIFE 80

MY PSYCHIATRIST IS GETTING RID OF HIS PATIENTS 81
MY PSYCHIATRIST HAS MYSTICAL EXPERIENCES 82
WE TALK ABOUT FALLING IN LOVE 83
MY PSYCHIATRIST DOESN'T UNDERSTAND ME 84
ALL YOU DO IS MAKE ME LAUGH 85
THE BIRTHDAY 86
LEARNING TO ACCEPT 87
LEARNING TO ACCEPT 2 88
FOR JUST A MOMENT 89
A CONVERSATION WITH GOD 90
MY PSYCHIATRIST CITES HIS PATIENT'S POEM 3 91
MY PSYCHIATRIST PAYS ME 92
THE GRANDEST ILLUSION 2 93

APPENDIX

BUT WHY DO I FEEL SO BAD 94
IN FEAR OF WITHDRAWAL SYMPTOMS 95
THE DANDYISM FIGHTS BACK 96
ON LOVE AGAIN 97
AND YET AGAIN ON ILLUSIONS 98
A CONVERSATION IN THE CEMETERY 99
AN INTERESTING SORT OF TOPIC 100
WELL FINALLY A BIT OF SEX 101
A CONVERSATION ABOUT JOURNEYS FARAWAY 102
AND THIS MORNING 103

ABOUT THE AUTHOR 104
ABOUT THE TRANSTATOR 105

THE WRITING ON THE WALL

A FEW WORDS CONCERNING
POEMS ABOUT MY PSYCHIATRIST

Charles S. Kraszewski

When Michał Zabłocki first turned my attention to Andrzej Kotański's verse cycle *Poems about my Psychiatrist* with the words 'a book of poetry that's outselling fiction,' my first (sincerely proud) reaction was *of course it is!* After all, how many times, over the years, have I argued that whereas poetry is the demesne of such a shrinking readership in America as to hardly merit the generous description of a 'niche market,' in Poland, my Poland, it is the *reader's choice.* I mean, Poland was the land of Mickiewicz and Słowacki in those sad years of partition, and of Miłosz and Herbert in the (arguably sadder) years of communist totalitarianism… Poland is the country where, to paraphrase Shelley, poets are the *acknowledged* legislators of the nation!

After all, who doesn't remember the lines of readers snaking down Basztowa St. in Kraków, queuing up to buy the newest offering from the pen of Jerzy Harasymowicz at the Pod Globusem bookstore on the corner of Basztowa and Długa?

But who am I kidding? Those queues evaporated somewhere around 1989. In 1990 Poland became a truly free, normal country; in 2004 a member of the European

Union, and a quick look at the most popular books at Empik (Poland's own version of Amazon) for the year 2019 will turn up titles like Christel Petitcollin's *How to Think Less*, Heather Morris's *The Tattooist of Auschwitz* and Donald Tusk's *Sincerely*, to name just three, none of which are poetry. Further down the line we find the Polish translation of Michelle Obama's *Becoming*. Having a look at the list of bestsellers from 2022 — which I revisited on account of the recent, celebratory reissue of Kotański's masterpiece — I must say that the first ten titles that appear there are, well, rather even less ambitious than the 2019 list. The first serious book appears in the tenth position: *World War III is Coming*, notable, on the one hand, for being a book written by Poles (whereas most of the top ten are translations of American pulp), but again, nothing to get too excited about.[1]

The most ambitious, in a literary sense, among the first ten or so books in the list of the one hundred best sellers of 2019 are several recent novels by Olga Tokarczuk. Now, although no one respects Tokarczuk's narrative talents more than I, one wonders how much those sales numbers were boosted by a certain prize she was awarded that year… and how many of those hastily purchased

---

1   As I write this introduction in March 2022, the title of this book seems eerily prescient. The publisher's blurb asks 'Is the world on the edge of nuclear annihilation?' — something that is on everyone's mind today, given the unjust and desperate war that Putin's Russia is waging against Ukraine; one in which the Russians, it seems, refuse to rule out the use of such horrible weapons 'if faced with existential threat.' And yet — you can't help chuckling — the authors, one of whom is described as a 'renowned geopolitical thinker,' were actually worried, last year, about 'whether the United States would go to war against China' and 'whose side would Russia take?' So much for prognosticators. Renowned or not.

copies of *Hemispheres* and *Drive your Plow over the Bones of the Dead* will be read cover to cover by those who bought them…? But more about Polish Nobel winners in a moment.

In short, Poland has become a normal western country, and the readers of Poland have acquired the usual tastes of readers of normal western countries, shaped by a now-unfettered book industry that dictates said tastes in a normal western way, in other words, by publishing what sells to the masses. Period.

Now, if anything, this state of things says even more about the achievement of Andrzej Kotański's *Poems about my Psychiatrist*. For if Poles have become a normal pulp-fiction, scandal-mongering, celebrity-stalking, self-help reading public (and Amazon statistics don't lie; yes, Amazon is in Poland too), how are we to explain the phenomenon of this book of verse? Still in print after ten years, and in the above-mentioned year of 2019 alone selling over 1100 copies (which translates into three people buying a copy every day)? As the author's publisher once remarked, 'As far as poetry is concerned, besides the Nobel winners, only Kotański sells.'

To anyone who really reads poetry for pleasure, the answer is a simple one. This is good poetry, very good poetry. To give just one example, from the first few pages of the book, let's have a look at 'My Psychiatrist Has Episodes of Fury:'

> because of the winter
> he says he froze to death during the Napoléonic wars
> and this is why he hates with equal passion
> Russia and frost
> war and walking
> so I advised him to forgive that particular incarnation

forgiveness ought to cure him of all his pain

but he says that it's difficult to forgive
l'Empereur

I get that

but who it is that I should be forgiving
there wasn't any time left to discuss

Kotański's poetry is characterised by the same lightness of touch that we find in the verse of Zbigniew Herbert — one of the most approachable, and yet deep, poets of the contemporary European idiom. It is a deceptively simple style, so lucid and pared to the bone as to be a perfect example of what Ezra Pound was talking about, when he said that poetry should strive to be as well written as prose. As in Herbert's verse, we find here direct statement, a subtle emotional charge, and a breadth of historical context which recalls the dilemma of Pan Cogito — the helpless individual, bravely confronting the steamrollers of power. But Kotański gives a special twist to the character of his witness to the world into which we are all thrust: the neurosis of contemporary western man. The poem ends with three simple lines, which are yet as powerful as a punch to the solar plexus: 'I get that / but who it is that I should be forgiving / there wasn't any time left to discuss.' This ironic, yet nerve-wracked exclamation would sound quite natural in the mouth of any of the protagonists played by Woody Allen. Is it this that makes the book popular, even amongst those readers who otherwise leave poetry behind them, once they emerge, relieved, from the Polish literature portion of their high school maturity exam?

The power of Herbert's sardonic verse arose from the manner in which it reacted to the oppressive communist junta he rejected and protested against. He lent a voice to the grey men and women of Polish society in the late twentieth century, who were faced with the same problems, historical and societal, as his great creation, the quixotic Pan Cogito. In one of his last interviews before his death, he lamented, only half-jokingly, the passing of that hated, Russian-imposed régime: 'Nowadays, I've got nothing to write about, save my illness.' It is almost a cliché to speak of the 'malaise of modern western man.' But even clichés are based on truth. Perhaps, in modern Poland, illnesses — real or imagined (and it is suggested that Kotański's narrator, like Woody Allen's characters, just might be a hypochondriac) — are the new oppressive reality of the middle and upper classes, where third-world problems have been elbowed aside by those of the first world? Pan Cogito belongs to the historical past. Kotański's unnamed patient is the spokesman for this generation of workaholic, underinsured, overmortgaged Poles, sweating in the rat-race along with us all, dealing with broken dreams, in relationships of various degrees of dysfunction.

If this is true, it can be comforting to no one. For what does it say of our society, if we are drawn to — perhaps recognise ourselves in? — the character of such a person, who finds himself in such a funk, that

> This inability to live as I would wish
> combined with my boredom with the life
> I have
> makes for vibrations of no high frequency

In his article 'Stressed Brits Buy Record Number of Self-Help Books' (*The Guardian*, 9 March 2019), Rob Walker tells us that

> Sales of self-help books have reached record levels in the past year, as stressed-out Britons turn to celebrities, psychologists and internet gurus for advice on how to cope with uncertain times. Three million such books were sold — a rise of 20% — according to figures from Nielsen Book Research, propelling self-improvement or pop psychology into one of the fastest-growing genres of publishing. [...] While the genre has tended to be more popular with women, Keira O'Brien, data editor at the *The Bookseller* magazine, said authors [...] had successfully wooed a younger, angst-ridden male audience. 'It's almost like male readers are looking for guidance or reassurance on how to be a man in a post #MeToo world,' O'Brien said. 'It's a noticeable skew which has never really happened before.'

The picture of the world that we are developing here is that of an atomised society — one in which human contact has been reduced to the minimum; in which social media have monopolised social interaction to such an extent that we are unsure of how to approach each other face to face. A progressive trend toward isolation is driving wedges between us, and our technology is certainly not helping matters any. Thinkers of such widely divergent backgrounds as the Anglo-Catholic T.S. Eliot and the militant atheist Jean-Paul Sartre are in agreement that isolation is the broad path to Hell. In Sartre's play *No Exit*, three characters, literally in Hell, might conceivably escape it, if only they could work together. Locked into their bickering individualities, however, co-operation is out of the question, and in Hell they shall remain. In Eliot's play *The Cocktail Party*, all of the main characters speed on their way to perdition as long as they remain separate, thinking only of themselves. They only succeed in pulling up at the last moment, avoiding the catastrophic ontological nosedive, when they re-integrate with others: Edward and Lavinia return to each other, and consciously strive to live as married couples should live; Celia enters the religious life, and gives her own life on behalf of others — finding, as her Master promised, an eternal life in return.

Quite similarly, what Kotański's narrator needs, at bottom, is not psychoanalysis, but love. The give-and-take, messy, devoted struggle in which one supports a real person, and is supported by him or her in return:

> if the internet
> contains all there is
> perhaps the internet
> created
> all there is

muses Kotański's patient — significantly contextualising his atomisation in the technology which has progressively overpowered our human world.

> all right
> but Agnieszka
> there's not a word to be found about her
> on the internet
>
> now you're starting to talk sense

It's not just that the psychiatrist prescribes good old-fashioned human interaction between man and woman as the cure-all to the patient's — real or imagined — problems. Deep down, that patient (Kotański's narrator) realises this to be the truth, himself. When asked if his wife is still living in New York, he replies:

> yes she still is
> on Grand St on the Lower East Side
>
> and you still love her
>
> so
> I was right
> you just want to piss me off

That 'and you still love her' comes at him, and us, with the same force as that punchline in the first poem quoted in this essay. He brushes it away, with anger, in the very manner of a person who knows it to be true, and is irritated at something he wished to be concealed being found out, stated baldly. So, depression. Kotański's narrator clings to depression as Linus clings to his security blanket. But the psychiatrist will have nothing of that:

> even the monks on Mount Athos
> get depressed
>
> *the world is in depression*
> *so are we*
>
> let's talk about Agnieszka

It all seems so simple. Perhaps it's a bit too simple. Besides his self-stated problems with women, Kotański's narrator is living out of joint in a city he would abandon in a minute, if he could, to return to his beloved Buenos Aires. That city — which the psychiatrist treats as a sort of *idée fixe*, an escapist rationalisation — presents itself again and again to the narrator's mind as a panacea. Until, near the end of the book:

> today I sighed
> Lord permit me to go back
> to Buenos Aires
>
> God responded
> sure

I bet he didn't expect that! But, well, really. What's stopping him? Yet here we run the risk of committing a fallacy of progression. Just because these verses — the Agnieszka prescription and God's benediction of his return to Argentina — occur near the end of the book, they are not necessarily the solution to the problem that comes before them. For Kotański's narrative does not proceed in a linear fashion, from statement of problem, through discussion of options, to solution. Although the cycle ends, quite literally, with a full stop,[2]

> I reckon that
> my grandest illusion
> is myself
>
> in comparison with that

---

[2] The first edition, that is. The second, 2022 version, includes the 'Appendix' of ten new poems, which extend the cycle.

> my psychiatrist is
> tiny
>
> teeny tiny
> o like
> this
> .

such a very self-assured statement, coming from such an unreliable source, prompts us to doubt it as a problematical claim, and returns us back to the text to wonder if we've missed anything. But all this does is muddle our picture of the narrator all the more. He is impenetrable, like any other human being (including, perhaps, ourselves), and his story is a messy one — just like real life.

Now, on the one hand, there is the self-help book and the psychoanalyst's couch, both of which (to speak, I know, ungenerously) are nothing but pleas for someone else to take control of our lives and tell us what to do. On the other, there is helping oneself, getting a grip on oneself, and taking responsibility for one's own life. Frustrated by his patient's inability to progress towards a cure (and by turns thankful for the same, for selfish reasons) the psychiatrist erupts at one point and challenges the moper:

> after all you could fly to Manhattan
> and go see Professor Girdwoyń
> or discontinue psychotherapy completely
> and make some appointments instead
> with an architect an interior decorator a supermodel
>   what do I know

So far, we've been talking about the popularity of *Poems about my Psychiatrist* from the perspective of the reader's identification with the narrator. But there might be another reason, too. Kotański's cycle is a humorous book, and part of its popularity might be its cathartic, not to say exorcistic, appeal, which allows the reader to laugh at the devil. Not identification with the narrator, but projection: an invitation to the reader to make use of the narrator as a scapegoat. 'At least I'm not in his shoes…' one might say, chuckling at the situations in which the narrator finds himself, and which he describes in so sardonic a tone as to encourage our laughter. Yet, keeping in mind the plight of Thomas Hardy's anguished agnostic narrator in 'The Impercipient:' 'O, doth a bird deprived of wings / go earth-bound willfully?' we can never overlook the extreme uniqueness of the individual human being — each and every one of us — something that, in another context, prompted Christ to challenge the know-it-alls surrounding the woman caught in adultery: 'Let him who is without sin cast the first stone.' So, is this simply a case of someone needing to 'get a grip on himself?' How can we be sure?

> I adore expressions like this
>
> you've got to finally recognise your potential
> you've got to finally appreciate yourself
> you've got to finally open up to people
> meet them half-way

the narrator complains, as if anticipating the question. Would a date with a supermodel or a chat with an interior decorator be just as helpful for the patient as these — expensive — sessions with a medical professional? We, as observers, have no right to pronounce upon the matter. We are in the position of a person walking down a city street and tossing a glance at the seemingly robust individuals who spend their days sitting on the sidewalk, begging for spare change. 'Why can't he just get a grip on himself, shave, and go look for a job? Any job?' the frustrated nine-to-fiver seethes, without it even crossing his mind that the person in question *isn't sitting there because he's lazy, or likes to*. He can't get up and 'do what I would do in his situation' because he is not 'me' and there is something quite wrong inside him, which prohibits him from doing what he would otherwise like to do himself. You don't have to toss a coin into his cup if you don't want to. But that said, you cannot make pronouncements about something, about someone, whom you do not know, and never will. Neither of Kotański's protagonists is really capable of understanding the other. Ironically, though, the psychiatrist may be correct, but *à rebours*:

> at this my psychiatrist says
> illusions illusions illusions
>
> he doesn't believe the slightest bit in the existence
> of real problems
> he believes only
> in the existence of illusory ones

A supermodel or an architect might be just as therapeutic and helpful for the suffering soul as a psychiatrist who will not recognise the reality of the patient's problem. It's easy, just as in our metaphor of the passer-by on the street with the indigent homeless, to say 'the voices you hear are just illusions!' (with the unsaid implication, *So deal with them!*); but, objectively real or not, the sufferer *still hears them*. It should be just as easy to treat the illusory voices as a *reality* that afflicts the sufferer, something that should lead the therapist to a real attempt to address the underlying *real* condition, which gives rise to them. But then he would run the risk of having to acknowledge — in pain, perhaps in horror — that there are some illnesses that cannot be cured, some 'illusory realities' that cannot be dealt with, talked away.

Speaking in terms of chess, the give-and-take of patient and psychiatrist in Kotański's cycle has reached stalemate. The narrator expresses this in a comical way, which is nonetheless full of tragic despair. When asked by the psychiatrist if euthanasia has ever crossed his mind, he replies:

> sometimes nothing crosses my mind at all
> but it once crossed my mind
> to name my daughter Euthanasia
>
> hmm
> what about your son
>
> him I'd probably like to name
> Jesus Mary and Joseph

The hopelessness of this situation, this utter lack of contact between the two human beings, is expressed in such pithy, sarcastic lines, characteristic of Kotański's poetics:

> have you never thought
> of finally
> giving this life of yours
> some direction
>
> no
> I've never thought of that

The psychiatrist — assuming that he truly does exist in the first place — is not being helpful with these platitudes of his. As we hint above, the only one deriving any advantage from this state of things is the psychiatrist himself. In the exchange below, the first stanza is spoken by the patient, the second by the therapist:

> it's atrociously stubborn and prolonged
> in fact as long as I can remember
> ever since I finished school
> and started my first job
> I've felt like this
>
> in other words
> we might say that
> your condition is stable

Can there be any better example of a disconnect?

To describe this 'pat' situation, as generously as possible, we would suggest that the therapist would have the patient take the reins of his problem in hand, yet the patient can neither see the reins, nor has he the strength to grab them, if he could. This results in a sad sort of comedy; the only 'solution' is to keep meeting, keep talking, keep… paying:

> for the love of God man
> you've not been put on this earth
> to fund my Caribbean vacations

We may choose to laugh at this, or not.

To return for a moment to Kotański and the craft of poetry, we have been so far discussing his prosody in terms of its sparseness, its Herbert-like pithiness of direct statement. This is true of the individual poems themselves. However, the cycle itself is an elaborately crafted whole in which the repetition of themes is used to subtly, yet effectively, underscore leitmotifs such as the gulf between patient and psychiatrist, which we have just been describing. For example, in flailing about — is there any other proper term? — for a therapy that would lead to a betterment of the patient's condition, the doctor contradicts himself:

> for the love of God man
> you've not been put on this earth
> to make an impression on your psychiatrist

he says, in the verse entitled with the first line of this fragment, only to state, apodictically, two poems on (in one of those uprushes of frustration — *Get a grip!*)

> all that you had to do was to come in
> and say you can kiss my ass
> make a good impression

To the patient's credit, at one point, he calls him out on this:

> and now you're telling me that
> my anima is not integrated
> and just a while ago you insisted
> that the so-called anima does not exist
>
> I didn't say that it doesn't exist
> only that its existence
> was never scientifically proven
> by Jung

super
so how am I supposed to integrate it
if such is the case

Form is content — otherwise, why would a writer choose to express himself in that most demanding form of human expression, poetry — and Kotański's mastery of form, here expressed in the carefully planned resumption of themes and contradictions, emphasises the key motif of the work: bewilderment, an attempt to grapple with a problem that is too great for anyone to tackle — the inner workings of the troubled soul.

The overarching form of the book: dialogue, analysis, is a trap expertly set by the author, to catch the reader in its toils. In engaging with this text, especially if we choose to distance ourselves from that 'scapegoat' of a narrator, we busy ourselves with analysis as well. However, before long it becomes apparent that this will be no easy task. As mentioned above, the form of the narrative is such that, arriving at the end, that eloquent full stop, we suddenly realise that it is no full stop at all. We are left hungry for more, for a solution, in search of which we loop back into the narrative, digging for clues that we have missed, and in this way, Kotański creates a continuum. However, the great human aspect of the work is made all the more strong thereby, for this is not a loop of frustration. In craftily forcing us back, again and again, to a consideration of what we've just read, Kotański is confronting us — again and again — with the human being of the narrator, challenging us to sympathy, challenging our sympathy. And it is a challenge to be sympathetic to a person who expresses himself in this manner:

> when I think of him there
> in the chicest boutiques of St Moritz
> outfitting himself in Bulgari gewgaws
>
> I get this overwhelming urge to fuck somebody up

Immediately, for this is the first poem in the collection, Kotański knocks our suppositions akilter by undercutting the moral quality of his patient. Are we to sympathise with him, as one of us, lost, angry at those who have power — real or imagined — over us, or fear him, as one of those horrid unknown variables that might one day walk into our post office and start shooting? Or then there's this dainty little fantasy, about coming across a little boy walking a dog:

> now if I grabbed the kid and
> strangled him
> his mama would run out into the street
> in tears
> and I could slide my hand
> beneath her skirt

There's absolutely nothing funny about that! Or, finally, the description of the patient's despairing, lonely drive through Warsaw, which leads him (of course!) past the building where the psychiatrist lives:

> of course I know
> that he exists
> because I took a drive along Śniegocka and saw
> the light burning on the second floor

Sympathy is all well and good, but can anyone feel sympathy for a stalker?

Of course, this last point is predicated on the given, that the psychiatrist actually exists. As we mentioned before, Kotański keeps us so off balance in his engrossing narrative of impenetrably complex modern humanity, that we can never be fully certain that the psychiatrist is anything more than a figment of the narrator's imagination, a second self, or an imaginary friend, created to be a sounding board. What do we have here? A dialogue, or just one narrative voice split into two? 'Your grandest illusion,' states the psychiatrist during one of these conversations (whether it is being held in an office, or in the narrator's own cranium),

> is that
> you're actually meeting with
> some sort of psychiatrist
>
> you understand me
> that is an illusion
>
> ill u si on

The soul of great art is ambiguity. One of the most effective examples of that is Goethe's ballad 'Erlkönig.' That little narrative is built up from four distinct voices: that of the omniscient narrator, that of the ailing child, that of the child's worried father, and finally, that of the Alder-king or Elf-king, who seeks to persuade the young boy to go off with him, into a land of endless game and song. The question that is forced upon the reader in the short stanzas of Goethe's poem concerns the nature of the Elf-king. Does he really exist, as a malignant spirit, seeking to tear the child's soul from his body? Or is he merely the figment of the agonising child's imagination, the hallucination that the father insists he is, as he tries to soothe his feverish child, as they gallop desperately toward safety? We cannot tell, as Goethe knocks us off balance by a subtle graphic artifice. When the father, or the child, speaks, their words are set off from the rest of the text by the preceding dash symbol, which designates direct speech. Of course, when the narrator is speaking, his words are unmarked. When the *Elf-king* speaks, his words are set off by quotation marks. They are, thus, a *tertium quid*, separate from both the narrator's descriptive words, and the direct speech of father and son. We cannot know, although a shiver suddenly shoots down the spine of the rationalist father in the last lines of the poem, as his son passes away… almost as if to signify a sudden doubt: *What if my son was right, seeing things, to which I am blind?* The answer to that question, if affirmative, stretches past the present, tragic moment to challenge the adult's entire world-view, developed and made firm over so many years.

In this way, Goethe expertly encapsulates the great quandary of his Europe: the so-called battle between the Classicists and the Romantics, and — arguably, inches over toward the Romantic camp, by at least admitting the possibility of the child's take on things, although (and this is the point) neither of the opposing claims can be definitively proven.

Another monument of tantalising ambiguity, written in our own day and age, in fact, nearly exactly contemporaneous to *Poems about my Psychiatrist*, is *Muerte en la rúa Augusta*, a verse novel by the Mexican poet Tedi López Mills. In that poem, the backstory of which begins with the nervous breakdown of Gordon, a grey little pencil pusher from Fullerton, California, nearly all of the information we receive about Gordon's daily life comes from Gordon himself, whose mind, as we have just mentioned, is unbalanced. Is his wife Donna a conniving, greedy adulteress, preying upon her weak husband? Or is she the innocent victim of his predatory excesses? Even the narrator will not help us here, as she restrains herself to didascalia. Even when she describes Gordon's actions and thought processes, she does so without comment: what we see, and hear, is what we get — what Gordon gives us.

Like Kotański's narrator, López Mills' Gordon is atomised, alone, lonely. And just as Kotański's narrator has a Psychiatrist — real or imaginary — to converse with, so in *Muerte en la rúa Augusta* we are introduced to the character of Anónimo, a 'friend' of whose material existence we are unsure. Can anyone else besides Gordon see him? Is he the creation of a mind condemned to solitude, or has he an independent existence, like some sort of evil spirit, possessing Gordon and pushing him away from the people he loves — Donna, Ralph, Don Jaime — people who might really aid him back to health? We cannot tell.

It is striking to set these creations in the context of the modern anti-heroes of the last one hundred years. We might begin with Jaroslav Hašek's Josef Švejk, that trickster who infuriates the powers that be in Austria, and who, through his sly clownery, always lands on his feet, and continue through those witnesses — mute or otherwise — of communist repression, such as Herbert's Pan Cogito, and 'N. N.' of Stanisław Barańczak's magnificent *Artificial Respiration*, to arrive at last at Gordon, and Kotański's troubled narrator. Who are these last two, but representatives of our modern culture, comfortable, seemingly benign, but rudderless, perhaps meaningless, who have no one to outsmart, no one to struggle against, but themselves?

Considering the ancient principle upon which all oppression is based: 'divide and conquer,' in Andrzej Kotański's narrator, we have a victim of just such division — the atomised individual, divided from the community of other men and women. And if — as is quite possible — his psychiatrist is nothing but 'illusion / ill u si on,' evidence of a split personality, we have here the most violent division of all, and a more resounding conquering of the individual human being than even the worst of the totalitarian states could dream up. If such is the case, we can only hope that the spectacular, well-deserved popularity of Andrzej Kotański's *Poems about my Psychiatrist* — and long may it last! — is indicative of the determination of its readership to heed the subtle, yet so profound, warnings it offers us.

*   *   *

The present translation, authorised by the poet, is based on the second, anniversary edition of the Polish original and includes the poems added to the cycle following the first printing. *Poems about my Psychiatrist* continues its triumphant progress through Polish culture. In August, 2021, an adaptation of the book for the stage under the title *Stan stabilny* [Condition Stable] was produced at the Teatr bez rzędów in Kraków, directed by Tadeusz Łomnicki.

Kraków — New York
22 December 2019 — 24 March 2022

MY PSYCHIATRIST WENT SKIING

he's in Chamonix or the Val d'Isère
I forget which

today I went for a walk along the tracks
thinking about my life again
the life I don't have

I can't quite come to terms with beet soup
beet soup pisses me off

I didn't call Iza for the umpteenth time
in general I don't call anybody
and it occurred to me that
women are like auto repair shops
it's hard to hook up with them
unless you call first

again I took a walk along the tracks
thinking again

when I think of him there
in the chicest boutiques of St Moritz
outfitting himself in Bulgari gewgaws

I get this overwhelming urge to fuck somebody up

MY PSYCHIATRIST HAD A CLAUSTROPHOBIC EPISODE

he didn't leave his house for a full week
because he was ashamed to admit it

of course I didn't notice anything
I noticed only that he'd changed his eyeglass frames
so that he'd look like a Jewish intellectual
and not some stupid goy
I thought

and he meanwhile in a sudden flush of panic
began to gnaw his nails nervously
under the table though
so as to throw me off the scent

MY PSYCHIATRIST HAS EPISODES OF FURY

because of the winter
he says he froze to death during the Napoléonic wars
and this is why he hates with equal passion
Russia and frost
war and walking

so I advised him to forgive that particular incarnation
forgiveness ought to cure him of all his pain

but he says that it's difficult to forgive
l'Empereur

I get that

but who it is that I should be forgiving
there wasn't any time left to discuss

MY PSYCHIATRIST HAS A LOT TO SAY TO ME

today again I couldn't get a word in edgewise
the whole hour long

MY PSYCHIATRIST SUMS UP BUENOS AIRES

I found the ideal place for me to live
the only problem is I can't live there
it's just as if I'd met the ideal woman
and couldn't marry her

an experience both dramatic and traumatic
which doesn't do much for my self-esteem
since I can't
that means that I'm a loser

This inability to live as I would wish
combined with my boredom with the life
I have
makes for vibrations of no high frequency

if I really try
not to notice it
I'll be better off

MY PSYCHIATRIST WON'T WRITE ME WORK-RELEASES

he says I ought to finally
learn to accept the here and now

and I say to him that the here and now
is always and everywhere after all
so *eo ipso* I don't really have
to learn to accept it in my place of work
where I find it hardest to learn anything

and both of us as usual are right
but only he has the rubber stamp
I don't

here and now though fortunately
he let himself be bribed
with a bottle of Tanqueray

MY PSYCHIATRIST'S MUMBLING

something under his breath
hard to make it out
I don't really blame him
for being hard to understand
but the longer that I don't understand
the more I blame him
for charging so much

and he says well this is a teaching moment
one should learn never to blame anyone
even if he charges too much
well bien alors
I have to sigh even in foreign tongues
I don't blame him
after all it's thanks to him isn't it
that I've learned to mumble under my breath
now just you watch me
someday I'll even learn how to charge too much

I SAY TO MYSELF

on my way to buy another bottle of wine

who's gonna be hung over tomorrow eh
you'll be surprised
how surprised you'll be

my psychiatrist just nods his head in silence
in deep silence

as if this were any of his business

MY PSYCHIATRIST SAYS

that I'm all closed up
that if I were more open
I'd be better off

but I meanwhile
cling to all my old traumas
my old conditioning
my habitual behaviour

but coming here each week
that's a habitual behaviour of mine too

well of course it is
but after all you could fly to Manhattan
and go see Professor Girdwoyń
or discontinue psychotherapy completely
and make some appointments instead
with an architect an interior decorator a supermodel
                                              what do I know

out of habit
I paid him this time too
all 320 złoty

YOU'VE GOT TO FINALLY

I adore expressions like this

you've got to finally recognise your potential
you've got to finally appreciate yourself
you've got to finally open up to people
meet them half-way

you've got to finally express your feelings
anger for example

I adore expressions like this
they don't piss me off they don't
not a bit
not an itty bit

not even an itty bitty bit

MY PSYCHIATRIST REPRISES HIS FAVOURITE THEME

and so what about that sex life of yours yeah nothing
I don't have anyone to do it with
well but there's still some women left in the world I think

some yeah for sure
but old and ugly ones don't turn me on
and young and pretty ones don't want me

the question is
why don't they want you

because I've got too low self-esteem

and there's your answer

ILLUSIONS ILLUSIONS ILLUSIONS

well I simply can't
write a dissertation
I've got to make a living
unfortunately

just like I simply can't
hook up with Karolina
because then she'd think I wanted
to hook up with her for sex
and she only interests me
as an example
of a very intelligent person
which is none too common these days

there are other things I simply can't do
like sell the Land Rover today
because first I ought to decide
what I'd like to buy for the money I'd get

and repair the suspension
and the driver's side door

at this my psychiatrist says
illusions illusions illusions

he doesn't believe the slightest bit in the existence
of real problems
he believes only
in the existence of illusory ones

MY PSYCHIATRIST CITES HIS PATIENT'S POEM

he went out for a walk with the dog
that little son of such a pretty mama
now if I grabbed the kid and
strangled him
his mama would run out into the street
in tears
and I could slide my hand
beneath her skirt

MY PSYCHIATRIST IS PLAYING WITH A DOG

he says that a dog feels more
understands more
than a person

he says that a dog
never goes to work
ever

and that he's able to love unconditionally
forever
all life long he's able to love
unconditionally
but a person never

but does that fucking dog pay you
does that fucking dog ever fucking pay you
320 złoty
I'd like to ask

but I don't want to intrude on them

RATE HIKE PAINFUL RATE HIKE

if you make some progress
we'll keep the rate as is

but if you won't make any progress
we'll raise the rate to 540
all right

NO NO NO that's not all right
that's absurd for Pete's sake that's
fucked-up too

all right then
so we'll split the difference
410

MY CONDITION IS STABLE

all right then
so it's not depression
it's a downswing of the mood
or
as you put it
despondency produced by unfulfillment
but all the same
it's atrociously stubborn and prolonged
in fact as long as I can remember
ever since I finished school
and started my first job
I've felt like this

in other words
we might say that
your condition is stable

FOR THE LOVE OF GOD MAN

he doesn't know that I'm recording him on my own
                                            dictaphone
just like he's recording me
and so he permits himself
the odd vulgarity

fuckin'-a you've really got to change your
                                   self-assessment
it's you who has to do it shit I say
stop trying to pull the wool over both our eyes
buying a fucking excursion to fucking Tokyo

for the love of God man
you've not been put on this earth
to make an impression on your psychiatrist

FOR THE LOVE OF GOD MAN 2

go someplace
take a stroll by the river for example
or sleep with some girl or other

for the love of God man
you've not been put on this earth
to fund my Caribbean vacations

RELATIONSHIP TO DADDY

and where does this need to impress people
                                            come from

dressing up in the most expensive La Martina
to show the world you know lingua latina

your relationship to your father must be
                                             dysfunctional

all that you had to do was to come in
and say you can kiss my ass
make a good impression

MY PSYCHIATRIST DOESN'T KNOW WHAT TO DO WITH ME

he says
I just already don't know
what I'm to do with you
anymore

how many times must I go on telling you
that your life isn't mega-shitty
but the mere fact that you so assess it
makes it so

how many times must I go on telling you
that the situation isn't the same thing
as the assessment of the situation

how many times must I go on telling you
that assessment is not the consequence of suffering
but that suffering is the consequence of assessment
how many times

and he broke down
and began sobbing
and took a trip to Namibia
to recover

MY PSYCHIATRIST PRETENDS THAT HE DOESN'T EXIST

doesn't reply to email
doesn't reply to texts
doesn't pick up the phone
since last Wednesday

of course I know
that he exists
because I took a drive along Śniegocka and saw
the light burning on the second floor
and if I'd waited a bit longer maybe
I'd've even caught him red-handed

but I couldn't wait any more
because lately I've been feeling bad
real bad
since last Wednesday

AN ADMISSION

I once lectured on diagnostics
at Harvard Medical School
ah this was
twenty two or even
twenty three years ago

I taught this seminar there
on hypochondria
in psychiatry
how I regret
not knowing you back then

MY GRANDEST ILLUSION

your grandest illusion
is that
you're actually meeting with
some sort of psychiatrist

you understand me
that is an illusion

ill u si on

RETURNING TO THE HERE AND NOW

your traumas all concern the past
and your meds all affect the future
the only thing that's here and now
is boredom

what does this boredom tell us
I ask you
well this boredom it tells us
that you simply aren't concentrating
on the here and now

once again your mind is miles from here
in Buenos Aires

RETURNING TO THE HERE AND NOW 2

we know that the future doesn't really exist
we know that the past doesn't really exist

now as wise and educated persons
cultural intelligent
we're not going to concern ourselves
with things that don't exist are we

what remains us
is the here and now

only I just can't drag you
into the here and now

because in your mind you're in Buenos Aires
de puta madre

MY PSYCHIATRIST LISTENS TO JAZZ

New York jazz
he says that New York jazz
needs more space

and so he's painted the walls a light grey
supposedly for better acoustics

whaddaya think
he asked

kind of sad

and that's just perfect
it's not the walls that should be happy

IMPATIENCE

stopped at a red light
fucking red light
I say
change already

and at that moment
I hear him
in my head
speaking in that educated
wiseass deep voice of his

it's not about the light changing
it's you who've got to change

THE FIRST CONVERSATION

Darth Vader was my father
and my mother was the Snow Queen
the unwanted child am I
of parents who didn't get along
and this is why I've suffered
my whole life through

everybody's had a rough childhood
literally
everyone

you should see my family

I DON'T KNOW WHAT THEY MEAN

said my psychiatrist
I don't know what they mean
these recurring thoughts of New York

maybe I'm getting messages
from somewhere beyond
since I'm constantly pulled and pulled
in that direction
or maybe some previous incarnations
I don't I just don't know

and maybe it's just snobbism
I think to myself

maybe it's a sign
that you ought to go there
I say

yes yes
it's probably a sign
says my suddenly cheery
psychiatrist

UNUSUAL NAMES

I can't figure out that beet soup
why it pisses me off that beet soup

does euthanasia ever cross your mind

sometimes nothing crosses my mind at all
but it once crossed my mind
to name my daughter Euthanasia

hmm
what about your son

him I'd probably like to name
Jesus Mary and Joseph

SYMPTOMS OF THE WANDERING REASON

sometimes you wander
from store to cinema
from cinema to store
from fiancée manquée to old boss
from doctorate to the attempt at emigration

have you never thought
of finally
giving this life of yours
some direction

no
I've never thought of that

REAL THERAPY REALLY

begins
when we start talking
at last
about that which is
and not about that
which is not

as if up till now
all we've been talking about
were illusions

RETURNING TO THE HERE AND NOW 3

my professional ethics
forbid me
from talking with you about something
that doesn't exist

now do you really think
that Buenos Aires exists

I mean really

DYSFUNCTIONAL EMANATIONS

because you don't emanate

neither love
nor charisma
nor positive energy

this is why
those women can't even see you

now what must happen
for you to emanate finally

how's that for an interesting topic

WHY

that's a good question
how do you feel about it

why don't you guess
there are so many places in the world
the Antilles
Cuba
New Caledonia
why am I here
where I least want to be

well, that question is worth 47 points
one for each year you've fucked up so far

NON-NEW YORK JAZZ

why are you listening to that
it doesn't sound like New York jazz at all

you're right
it's actually
non-New York jazz
my psychiatrist blushed

I shot him a meaningful look
and he blushed all the more

It's a demo I've got to listen to
by a patient of mine
he lied

it was a pleasant feeling
to realise that I wasn't the only one
who had to lie during therapy

but then it made me sad of a sudden
which I did my best to conceal

only later
when I was alone
did I help myself with a glass of Armagnac
listening to whatever

MY LUCIFERISM

this snobbism elitism
this love of luxury
self-elevation and lack of humility
this stubbornness
acting out in spite of everything
and everybody
and in the face of obvious facts
all points plainly to
luciferist influences
in your personality
alas

ok
but even so
I'd sooner deny Christ
Our Lord and His Holy Mother
Immaculately Conceived
than my dreams

and all this is being recorded

MY PROMISCUITY

o no
that's not sick
no
rather what's sick
is your strange stubborn
obsession with monogamy

while after all
one might
one is allowed to
it's much better to
copulate with many partners
like a chimp like a bonobo

but there you go
bobo
oh
no no
this Catholic upbringing of yours
has perverted your outlook
alas

MY ANIMA

and now you're telling me that
my anima is not integrated
and just a while ago you insisted
that the so-called anima does not exist

I didn't say that it doesn't exist
only that its existence
was never scientifically proven
by Jung

super
so how am I supposed to integrate it
if such is the case

that nobody knows
the integration of scientifically
unsubstantiated archetypes
is the greatest challenge
in psychiatry

MY EVERYDAY DANDYISM

today
I see that you've dressed yourself up
in the immortal style of the 80s

yes
I liked the 1980s
there was a lot of sun back then
everything seemed possible
there were so many dreams back then to realise

and now

now
the only dreams I have left
are suicidal

hmm
I'd rather you dreamed
of winning the lottery
the visualisation is more pleasant
and the chances of fulfilment are the same

EVERYDAY DANDYISM 2

well today I see you've dressed yourself
with unconditional unconcern

I rather had in mind the style
of a *bonbon vivant*

well congratulations
who are you trying to fool
with a look like that

myself for sure
but you no
as for everybody else
ah
they're all wrapped up
in their own looks

CORTE DEL LUGANEGHER

there's only one passage
from the world of luciferist illusion
to the world of divine truth
do you know where it's found

well no I don't
but knowing you
I reckon that it's
in the here and now

you're wrong
it's to be found in Venice
in a little dead end street
near the Corte del Luganegher

but to pass through it
you absolutely need
an ally
optimally your totem animal
in your case
that would be the black panther

wait
are you being serious

no
I was joking

WE TALK ABOUT QUANTUM PHYSICS

the world's really not the way it is
it's not what it seems to us to be
to tell the truth
the world doesn't actually exist

you mean to say
that it's all an illusion

this time no
this time I'm saying
that all of this so-called reality of ours
well ninety-six percent of it
is comprised of the void
and only four percent
is illusion

and you're saying that with a straight face

this time yeah

PITY PARTY

people have wives children
fourteen grandchildren
cats dogs scooters
while I
I'm not even able to give that Marta a call
although I was so head over heels for her
so tell me huh
why is that

well
I'll tell you

everybody is different
but you sir are even more different
than everybody

MY PSYCHIATRIST GOES A-HUNTING

he's very proud of himself
they invited him to Yorkshire
for a gala hunt of the fox
he's even bought himself
a Harris Tweed

there'll be over a hundred people there
four dozen dogs
and then a banquet
and then a booze-up
and cetera

don't you feel sorry for the fox
I asked him

he was silent for a moment
and then he said
I feel sorry for you

WE TALK ABOUT LIFE

and so it's like this
your sex life is a failure
your professional life is too
to say nothing of your social life
failure again
is there any other life left you
to ruin

life after death

WE TALK ABOUT DEATH

all of this auto-destruction of yours
all of these bad habits
all of this acting against your own best interests
doing what you don't want to do
not doing what you do want to do
what do you think
what does all this say to us

that I want to die

everybody wants to die
that's why everybody dies

WE TALK ABOUT THE INTERNET

if the internet
contains all there is
perhaps the internet
created
all there is
we don't know
and maybe
we'll never find out

all right
but Agnieszka
there's not a word to be found about her
on the internet

now you're starting to talk sense

WE TALK ABOUT LOVE

were you ever in love
I mean really

sure
I love my mustard jar
I found it in my grandmother's garden
I washed it
brought it to Warsaw
I love it so much
I've even kissed it several times
out of love

fascinating
said my psychiatrist

MY PSYCHIATRIST CITES HIS PATIENT'S POEM 2

I drink a bit
a bit
a bottle
two

but not like back then
when I was young
to the dregs
to the break of dawn
until I passed out

o no not that

WE TALK ABOUT MY EX-WIFE

your ex-wife
she still lives in New York

she wasn't my wife
she was merely one of my illusions

ok
got it
but she still lives there right

why do you keep asking to piss me off
or just to edge that topic in again New York

I'm only asking if she's still living there

yes she still is
on Grand St on the Lower East Side

and you still love her

so
I was right
you just want to piss me off

MY PSYCHIATRIST IS GETTING RID OF HIS PATIENTS

chucked four so far
he tells me today
with the smile of some
freeloading son of a bitch

but you no
I'm holding on to you

because it's amusing
really

how you're not improving at all

MY PSYCHIATRIST HAS MYSTICAL EXPERIENCES

recently it was the Genius of Freedom that appeared
                                                                       to him
before that it was the archangel Azrael
and earlier still
the great angel of Cuernavaca

now this is the man who
when we're talking about my problems
calls them illusions

I don't know how I'm supposed to deal with this
most likely
he's trying to provoke me
into saying
will you finally cut it out
with all that bullshit

but I won't let him provoke me
that's not what I'm paying him for

WE TALK ABOUT FALLING IN LOVE

you only fall in love really
when you start
taking codeine

then you can fall in love
with the greyness of the walls
with the transparency of water
with a leaf with an ashtray

but everything that you've been talking about
that's all just illusions

ok
so maybe you can prescribe me
some of that codeine

I can
but I really don't want to
I really really don't want to
I don't want you to really fall in love

because from my psychiatric point of view
your illusions are a lot more interesting

MY PSYCHIATRIST DOESN'T UNDERSTAND ME

I don't understand you
he says
I don't understand you
at all
how can you endure so many years
in an advertising agency
and how can you endure so many years
in a completely failed relationship
with yourself
how can you not love yourself to such a degree
as to condemn yourself to unending
companionship with a person
that you don't love
no
this I'll never be able to understand
no no no
I can understand many things
but this no this no way

but for Pete's sake
I've explained it all to him
more than once

ALL YOU DO IS MAKE ME LAUGH

when you say
that you're depressed
all you do is make me laugh
really
everyone gets depressed
everyone
the employees of multibillion dollar companies
get depressed
and the faithful of various denominations
get depressed
even the monks on Mount Athos
get depressed

the world is in depression
so are we

let's talk about Agnieszka

THE BIRTHDAY

what should I buy you
for your birthday
I asked my doctor

wine
said my doctor

so now let's just think that through
what sort of wine
if I buy him good expensive wine
he'll say it's snobbism
luciferism

if I buy cheap wine
the diagnosis will be
that I have too low self-esteem

and if I don't show up at all
he'll conclude that
I'm introverted
suffering from various phobia
maybe even misanthropy
which actually hits the nail right on the head

and so I won't show up
but I will drink the wine

the expensive one rather

LEARNING TO ACCEPT

when will you finally be able
to accept your job
to accept your place on this earth
that is your native land
and to go even further
to accept yourself
oh then we'll finally
be able to put the proper foot forward

yeah but I
will never be able
to accept all of that
never never ever

and that's why you need a psychiatrist

LEARNING TO ACCEPT 2

now what must happen
for you to begin accepting yourself

well I'd have to be
exactly what I'm not

great
in other words we can make a date
when will you be like that

well not tomorrow
but maybe never
how does never strike you

FOR JUST A MOMENT

let's say that you win
those seventeen millions
what'll you do

I'll fly off
to Buenos Aires
to San Francisco
to New Zealand

of course
in other words
escapism

A CONVERSATION WITH GOD

today I sighed
Lord permit me to go back
to Buenos Aires

God responded
sure

MY PSYCHIATRIST CITES HIS PATIENT'S POEM 3

Monday Tuesday Wednesday
about those what is there to say
but on Thursday
you're thinking about the weekend

after which it all begins again

MY PSYCHIATRIST PAYS ME

so he said

I know it doesn't matter to you
if you get well or not
but it really matters to me
to achieve another therapeutical success

so can we come to this sort of arrangement
now you won't be paying me
I'll be paying you for each session

well how much
I asked him

360

I shook my head
and then I said
400

THE GRANDEST ILLUSION 2

and I reckon that
my grandest illusion
is myself

in comparison with that
my psychiatrist is
tiny

teeny tiny
o like
this
.

APPENDIX

BUT WHY DO I FEEL SO BAD

maybe they're putting toxins
into the cigarettes
or the alcohol
to weaken my love of life

no
I don't think so no
never heard anything like that

but what'm I supposed to do about it

well I could suggest a lobotomy

or a placebo
third generation
very effective

IN FEAR OF WITHDRAWAL SYMPTOMS

abstinence to put it quite simply is very boring
after the first two or three jolts of euphoria
it's hard to maintain the enthusiasm day after day
that you're no longer drinking no longer using

we've got to think up some further deprivations

o of course
we've gotten rid of alcohol
we've gotten rid of drugs
now we'll get rid of meds
and here come the heebie jeebies

o please let's not be
so afraid of the heebie jeebies
from the very dawn of history
no one's ever been harmed by the heebie jeebies

THE DANDYISM FIGHTS BACK

but this new style of yours
how exactly am I to interpret that

I dress in bright colours
so no one will catch on to the fact
that I'm dying

well you know
life in general
tends towards death
and even the loudest trousers
won't change that

I know
when you're over forty
you're already a corpse
but you see the trick is
to be a lively corpse

ON LOVE AGAIN

now has anyone ever loved you

well if it's women you mean
no rather not
but if we take into consideration
for example
those Three Divine Persons
well then we can't
count them out

maybe even
Our Lady of Częstochowa loved me

but she did her best
not to show it

AND YET AGAIN ON ILLUSIONS

and your ex-wife

she doesn't live there any more
she's moved to Ireland now
which is somewhat odd
if you recall
that she was just an illusion of mine
can illusions pick up stakes and move somewhere

o my dear sir
they can do so much really
they are much more powerful than we realise

A CONVERSATION IN THE CEMETERY

and last weekend
I went off to Powązki
to have a chat with my great-grandfather

now that's interesting
and what did he tell you

he told me to quit smoking

and you did

ehh
should I let on old windbag like that poison me

AN INTERESTING SORT OF TOPIC

at Harvard Medical School
which I've mentioned so many times
they taught us rather to
avoid polemicising with our patients
it's better to go along with them

why are you telling me this

o well that you should understand
what'll be in my mind when I say
that you're right without a doubt right
as far as that Patrycja is concerned

and when will you stop making fun of me

just as soon as you start bringing me
something more interesting to talk about
than falling in love

WELL FINALLY A BIT OF SEX

no
I really think not
it'll only be a first date

very good
that's the very best time for it

you know why a person your age
ought to have sex on the first date

because he might not live to see a second one

A CONVERSATION ABOUT JOURNEYS FARAWAY

I'm attracted by exotic-sounding names
like Buprenorphine Oxycodone
Fentanyl Lorafen Xanax

that's nothing but kidney breakdown
and addiction
you can achieve the same results with alcohol

maybe maybe
but up till now it's done nothing for me

gimme the prescription
gimme

AND THIS MORNING

when I was sitting on the balcony
the Holy Spirit flew right up
in the shape of a dove
and shat on me

and what might that mean

well you know
there are some mysteries
that cannot be explained
with the aid of psychiatry

ABOUT THE AUTHOR

Andrzej Kotański, once called 'a star waiting to be discovered' by Biblioteka Kraków, is creative in poetry, prose, drama and the sung word. He debuted in 1990 with a collection of short stories entitled *Czterdzieści siedem tysięcy bankietów* [Forty-Seven Thousand Banquets], and since then has brought out three volumes of verse: *Elegia o płaszczu skórzanym* [An Elegy of a Leather Jacket, 1992], *Jutro będzie wiosna* [Tomorrow Will Be Spring, 1994] and *Wiersze o mom psychiatrze* [Poems about my Psychiatrist, 2011], the entirety of which is translated here into English. Kotański is the author of one play *Wersalka* [The Couch, 2000], and has composed many original songs in Polish, as well as translating songs from Italian, Spanish, French, English and Russian. Having studied Romance languages and literatures at the University of Warsaw (his master's thesis is a close reading of the French poetry of Rainer Maria Rilke), he has worked at the Institut Français in Warsaw, and also in advertising.

ABOUT THE TRANSLATOR

Charles S. Kraszewski is a poet and translator, creative in both English and Polish. He is the author of three volumes of original verse in English (*Diet of Nails; Beast; Chanameed*); two in Polish (*Hallo, Sztokholm*; *Skowycik*) and a farcical novel about the end of the world as we know it (*Accomplices, You Ask?*). He translates from Polish, Czech and Slovak into English, and from English and Spanish into Polish. He is a member of the Union of Polish Writers Abroad (London) and of the Association of Polish Writers (SPP, Kraków).

DRAMATIC WORKS
by Cyprian Kamil Norwid

'Perhaps some day I'll disappear forever,' muses the master-builder Psymmachus in Cyprian Kamil Norwid's *Cleopatra and Caesar,* 'Becoming one with my work…' Today, exactly two hundred years from the poet's birth, it is difficult not to hear Norwid speaking through the lips of his character. The greatest poet of the second phase of Polish Romanticism, Norwid, like Gerard Manley Hopkins in England, created a new poetic idiom so ahead of his time, that he virtually 'disappeared' from the artistic consciousness of his homeland until his triumphant rediscovery in the twentieth century.

Chiefly lauded for his lyric poetry, Norwid also created a corpus of dramatic works astonishing in their breadth, from the Shakespearean *Cleopatra and Caesar* cited above, through the mystical dramas *Wanda and Krakus, the Unknown Prince...*

Buy it > www.glagoslav.com

THE SONNETS

by Adam Mickiewicz

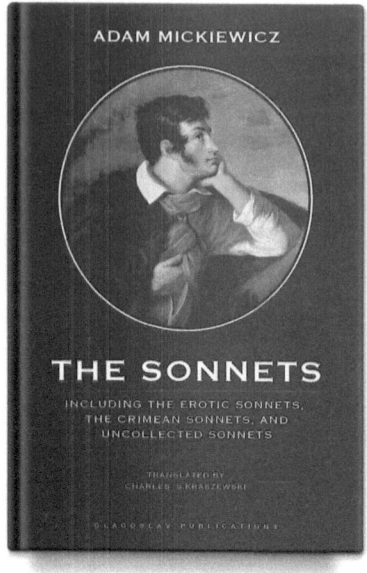

Because the poetry of Adam Mickiewicz is so closely identified with the history of the Polish nation, one often reads him as an institution, rather than a real person. In the *Crimean and Erotic Sonnets* of the national bard, we are presented with the fresh, real, and striking poetry of a living, breathing man of flesh and blood. Mickiewicz proved to be a master of Petrarchan form. His *Erotic Sonnets* chronicle the development of a love affair from its first stirrings to its disillusioning denouement, at times in a bitingly sardonic tone. *The Crimean Sonnets*, a verse account of his journeys through the beautiful Crimean Peninsula, constitute the most perfect cycle of descriptive sonnets since du Bellay. *The Sonnets* of Adam Mickiewicz are given in the original Polish, in facing-page format, with English verse translations by Charles S. Kraszewski. Along with the entirety of the Crimean and Erotic Sonnets, other "loose" sonnets by Mickiewicz are included, which provide the reader with the most comprehensive collection to date of Mickiewicz's sonneteering. Fronted with a critical introduction, *The Sonnets* of Adam Mickiewicz also contain generous textual notes by the poet and the translator.

Buy it > www.glagoslav.com

A BURGLAR OF THE BETTER SORT
by Tytus Czyżewski

The history of Poland, since the eighteenth century, has been marked by an almost unending struggle for survival. From 1795 through 1945, she was partitioned four times by her stronger neighbours, most of whom were intent on suppressing if not eradicating Polish culture. It is not surprising, then, that much of the great literature written in modern Poland has been politically and patriotically engaged. Yet there is a second current as well, that of authors devoted above all to the craft of literary expression, creating 'art for art's sake,' and not as a didactic national service. Such a poet is Tytus Czyżewski, one of the chief, and most interesting, literary figures of the twentieth century. Growing to maturity in the benign Austrian partition of Poland, and creating most of his works in the twenty-year window of authentic Polish independence stretching between the two world wars, Czyżewski is an avant-garde poet, dramatist and painter who popularised the new approach to poetry established in France by Guillaume Apollinaire, and was to exert a marked influence on such multi-faceted artists as Tadeusz Kantor.

Buy it > www.glagoslav.com

FOREFATHERS' EVE
by Adam Mickiewicz

Forefathers' Eve [*Dziady*] is a four-part dramatic work begun circa 1820 and completed in 1832 – with Part I published only after the poet's death, in 1860. The drama's title refers to *Dziady*, an ancient Slavic and Lithuanian feast commemorating the dead. This is the grand work of Polish literature, and it is one that elevates Mickiewicz to a position among the "great Europeans" such as Dante and Goethe.

With its Christian background of the Communion of the Saints, revenant spirits, and the interpenetration of the worlds of time and eternity, *Forefathers' Eve* speaks to men and women of all times and places. While it is a truly Polish work – Polish actors covet the role of Gustaw/Konrad in the same way that Anglophone actors covet that of Hamlet – it is one of the most universal works of literature written during the nineteenth century. It has been compared to Goethe's Faust – and rightfully so...

Buy it > www.glagoslav.com

OLANDA

by Rafał Wojasiński

I've been happy since the morning. Delighted, even. Everything seems so splendidly transient to me. That dust, from which thou art and unto which thou shalt return — it tempts me. And that's why I wander about these roads, these woods, among the nearby houses, from which waft the aromas of fried pork chops, chicken soup, fish, diapers, steamed potatoes for the pigs; I lose my eye-sight, and regain it again. I don't know what life is, Ola, but I'm holding on to it. Thus speaks the narrator of Rafał Wojasiński's novel *Olanda*. Awarded the prestigious Marek Nowakowski Prize for 2019, *Olanda* introduces us to a world we glimpse only through the window of our train, as we hurry from one important city to another: a provincial world of dilapidated farmhouses and sagging apartment blocks, overgrown cemeteries and village drunks; a world seemingly abandoned by God — and yet full of the basic human joy of life itself.

Buy it > www.glagoslav.com

GŁOSY / VOICES
by Jan Polkowski

In December 1970, amid a harsh winter and an even harsher economic situation, the ruling communist regime in Poland chose to drastically raise prices on basic foodstuffs. Just before the Christmas holidays, for example, the price of fish, a staple of the traditional Christmas Eve meal, rose nearly 20%. Frustrated citizens took to the streets to protest, demanding the repeal of the price-hikes. Things took an especially dramatic turn in the northern regions near the Baltic shore — later, the cradle of the Solidarity movement, which would eventually spark the fall of communism in Poland and throughout Central and Eastern Europe — where the government moved against their citizens with the Militia and the Army. Forty-one Poles were murdered by their own government when militiamen and soldiers opened fire with live rounds on the crowds in Gdańsk, Gdynia, Szczecin and Elbląg.

Jan Polkowski's moving poetic cycle *Głosy* [Voices], presented here in its entirety in the English translation of C.S. Kraszewski, is a poetic monument to the dead, their families, and all who were affected by the 'December Events,' as they are sometimes euphemistically referred to.

A BILINGUAL EDITION

Buy it > www.glagoslav.com

Glagoslav Publications Catalogue

- *The Time of Women* by Elena Chizhova
- *Andrei Tarkovsky: A Life on the Cross* by Lyudmila Boyadzhieva
- *Sin* by Zakhar Prilepin
- *Hardly Ever Otherwise* by Maria Matios
- *Khatyn* by Ales Adamovich
- *The Lost Button* by Irene Rozdobudko
- *Christened with Crosses* by Eduard Kochergin
- *The Vital Needs of the Dead* by Igor Sakhnovsky
- *The Sarabande of Sara's Band* by Larysa Denysenko
- *A Poet and Bin Laden* by Hamid Ismailov
- *Zo Gaat Dat in Rusland* (Dutch Edition) by Maria Konjoekova
- *Kobzar* by Taras Shevchenko
- *The Stone Bridge* by Alexander Terekhov
- *Moryak* by Lee Mandel
- *King Stakh's Wild Hunt* by Uladzimir Karatkevich
- *The Hawks of Peace* by Dmitry Rogozin
- *Harlequin's Costume* by Leonid Yuzefovich
- *Depeche Mode* by Serhii Zhadan
- *Groot Slem en Andere Verhalen* (Dutch Edition) by Leonid Andrejev
- *METRO 2033* (Dutch Edition) by Dmitry Glukhovsky
- *METRO 2034* (Dutch Edition) by Dmitry Glukhovsky
- *A Russian Story* by Eugenia Kononenko
- *Herstories, An Anthology of New Ukrainian Women Prose Writers*
- *The Battle of the Sexes Russian Style* by Nadezhda Ptushkina
- *A Book Without Photographs* by Sergey Shargunov
- *Down Among The Fishes* by Natalka Babina
- *disUNITY* by Anatoly Kudryavitsky
- *Sankya* by Zakhar Prilepin
- *Wolf Messing* by Tatiana Lungin
- *Good Stalin* by Victor Erofeyev
- *Solar Plexus* by Rustam Ibragimbekov
- *Don't Call me a Victim!* by Dina Yafasova
- *Poetin* (Dutch Edition) by Chris Hutchins and Alexander Korobko

- *A History of Belarus* by Lubov Bazan
- *Children's Fashion of the Russian Empire* by Alexander Vasiliev
- *Empire of Corruption: The Russian National Pastime* by Vladimir Soloviev
- *Heroes of the 90s: People and Money. The Modern History of Russian Capitalism* by Alexander Solovev, Vladislav Dorofeev and Valeria Bashkirova
- *Fifty Highlights from the Russian Literature* (Dutch Edition) by Maarten Tengbergen
- *Bajesvolk* (Dutch Edition) by Michail Chodorkovsky
- *Dagboek van Keizerin Alexandra* (Dutch Edition)
- *Myths about Russia* by Vladimir Medinskiy
- *Boris Yeltsin: The Decade that Shook the World* by Boris Minaev
- *A Man Of Change: A study of the political life of Boris Yeltsin*
- *Sberbank: The Rebirth of Russia's Financial Giant* by Evgeny Karasyuk
- *To Get Ukraine* by Oleksandr Shyshko
- *Asystole* by Oleg Pavlov
- *Gnedich* by Maria Rybakova
- *Marina Tsvetaeva: The Essential Poetry*
- *Multiple Personalities* by Tatyana Shcherbina
- *The Investigator* by Margarita Khemlin
- *The Exile* by Zinaida Tulub
- *Leo Tolstoy: Flight from Paradise* by Pavel Basinsky
- *Moscow in the 1930* by Natalia Gromova
- *Laurus* (Dutch edition) by Evgenij Vodolazkin
- *Prisoner* by Anna Nemzer
- *The Crime of Chernobyl: The Nuclear Goulag* by Wladimir Tchertkoff
- *Alpine Ballad* by Vasil Bykau
- *The Complete Correspondence of Hryhory Skovoroda*
- *The Tale of Aypi* by Ak Welsapar
- *Selected Poems* by Lydia Grigorieva
- *The Fantastic Worlds of Yuri Vynnychuk*
- *The Garden of Divine Songs and Collected Poetry of Hryhory Skovoroda*
- *Adventures in the Slavic Kitchen: A Book of Essays with Recipes* by Igor Klekh
- *Seven Signs of the Lion* by Michael M. Naydan

- *Forefathers' Eve* by Adam Mickiewicz
- *One-Two* by Igor Eliseev
- *Girls, be Good* by Bojan Babić
- *Time of the Octopus* by Anatoly Kucherena
- *The Grand Harmony* by Bohdan Ihor Antonych
- *The Selected Lyric Poetry Of Maksym Rylsky*
- *The Shining Light* by Galymkair Mutanov
- *The Frontier: 28 Contemporary Ukrainian Poets - An Anthology*
- *Acropolis: The Wawel Plays* by Stanisław Wyspiański
- *Contours of the City* by Attyla Mohylny
- *Conversations Before Silence: The Selected Poetry of Oles Ilchenko*
- *The Secret History of my Sojourn in Russia* by Jaroslav Hašek
- *Mirror Sand: An Anthology of Russian Short Poems*
- *Maybe We're Leaving* by Jan Balaban
- *Death of the Snake Catcher* by Ak Welsapar
- *A Brown Man in Russia* by Vijay Menon
- *Hard Times* by Ostap Vyshnia
- *The Flying Dutchman* by Anatoly Kudryavitsky
- *Nikolai Gumilev's Africa* by Nikolai Gumilev
- *Combustions* by Srđan Srdić
- *The Sonnets* by Adam Mickiewicz
- *Dramatic Works* by Zygmunt Krasiński
- *Four Plays* by Juliusz Słowacki
- *Little Zinnobers* by Elena Chizhova
- *We Are Building Capitalism! Moscow in Transition 1992-1997* by Robert Stephenson
- *The Nuremberg Trials* by Alexander Zvyagintsev
- *The Hemingway Game* by Evgeni Grishkovets
- *A Flame Out at Sea* by Dmitry Novikov
- *Jesus' Cat* by Grig
- *Want a Baby and Other Plays* by Sergei Tretyakov
- *Mikhail Bulgakov: The Life and Times* by Marietta Chudakova
- *Leonardo's Handwriting* by Dina Rubina
- *A Burglar of the Better Sort* by Tytus Czyżewski
- *The Mouseiad and other Mock Epics* by Ignacy Krasicki
- *Ravens before Noah* by Susanna Harutyunyan

- *An English Queen and Stalingrad* by Natalia Kulishenko
- *Point Zero* by Narek Malian
- *Absolute Zero* by Artem Chekh
- *Olanda* by Rafał Wojasiński
- *Robinsons* by Aram Pachyan
- *The Monastery* by Zakhar Prilepin
- *The Selected Poetry of Bohdan Rubchak: Songs of Love, Songs of Death, Songs of the Moon*
- *Mebet* by Alexander Grigorenko
- *The Orchestra* by Vladimir Gonik
- *Everyday Stories* by Mima Mihajlović
- *Slavdom* by Ľudovít Štúr
- *The Code of Civilization* by Vyacheslav Nikonov
- *Where Was the Angel Going?* by Jan Balaban
- *De Zwarte Kip* (Dutch Edition) by Antoni Pogorelski
- *Głosy / Voices* by Jan Polkowski
- *Sergei Tretyakov: A Revolutionary Writer in Stalin's Russia* by Robert Leach
- *Opstand* (Dutch Edition) by Władysław Reymont
- *Dramatic Works* by Cyprian Kamil Norwid
- *Children's First Book of Chess* by Natalie Shevando and Matthew McMillion
- *Precursor* by Vasyl Shevchuk
- *The Vow: A Requiem for the Fifties* by Jiří Kratochvil
- *De Bibliothecaris* (Dutch edition) by Mikhail Jelizarov
- *Subterranean Fire* by Natalka Bilotserkivets
- *Vladimir Vysotsky: Selected Works*
- *Behind the Silk Curtain* by Gulistan Khamzayeva
- *The Village Teacher and Other Stories* by Theodore Odrach
- *Duel* by Borys Antonenko-Davydovych
- *War Poems* by Alexander Korotko
- *Ballads and Romances* by Adam Mickiewicz
- *The Revolt of the Animals* by Wladyslaw Reymont
- *Liza's Waterfall: The hidden story of a Russian feminist* by Pavel Basinsky
- *Biography of Sergei Prokofiev* by Igor Vishnevetsky

More coming . . .

GLAGOSLAV PUBLICATIONS
www.glagoslav.com

www.ingramcontent.com/pod-product-compliance
Lightning Source LLC
Chambersburg PA
CBHW030306100526
44590CB00012B/536